PICTORIAL MELBOURN

A walk through Melbourn's past

Published by Melbourn Village History Group
Melbourn, Cambridge, England.

Printed 2004

© Melbourn Village History Group 2004

Acknowledgements
We are grateful to the Cambridge County Archives and the
Cambridgeshire Collection for their help and contribution
to this book.

Concept, design and production Peter & Jan Simmonett

Printed by The Burlington Press, Foxton, Cambridge.

ISBN 0-9549120-0-4

Contents

Introduction

This book has been planned to give an insight into Melbourn as it appeared years ago. It takes the reader through the village from the southern end – along the High Street, diverting along each of the lanes as they are encountered – returning to the High Street again, until the northern end of the village is reached.

Despite the revolutionary processes now evolving in modern photographic technology, the quality of some of the very early photographs, included in this publication, can still match that of today. An excellent example is our earliest known picture, on page 133, of the church *c*.1865. The clarity is extraordinary, the enlargement allowing us to see the expressions on the faces of the two men featured at the gate and at the porch.

The condition in which many of the photographs were received has been excellent. A few were blurred when taken, but nevertheless have been included here for their charm, period character and of course, photographic evidence. Others were torn or creased, or the image barely discernible but, with modern technology some of these pictures have been greatly improved and restored. See page 239.

We hope you enjoy this book, and the many treasures it holds, as much as we have enjoyed collecting and preserving the photographs for future generations.

Special thanks must go to all those who have contributed to this book – unfortunately, too many to list – and those who have spent many hours helping us to check the facts.

We have endeavoured to ensure that all the photographs displayed in this book are dated accurately and appear in sequence, although not in chronological order. However, it must be remembered that, as many of the buildings were demolished before the 1940s, verifying some of the sites has been a difficult task and therefore, there may be a few inaccuracies. Indications as to the content of the photographs were supplied by the contributors, or provided and checked by older members of the village. Any further information will be welcomed by The Melbourn Village History Group.

The Melbourn Village History Group

ANN DEKKERS, PETER DEKKERS, MAVIS HOWARD,
ERIC JOHNSTON, COLIN LIMMING, TERRY ROLT,
JAN SIMMONETT, PETER SIMMONETT, MARY WOODCOCK,
SALLY WRIGHT WITH RAY ELLIS AND DAPHNE BLACK.

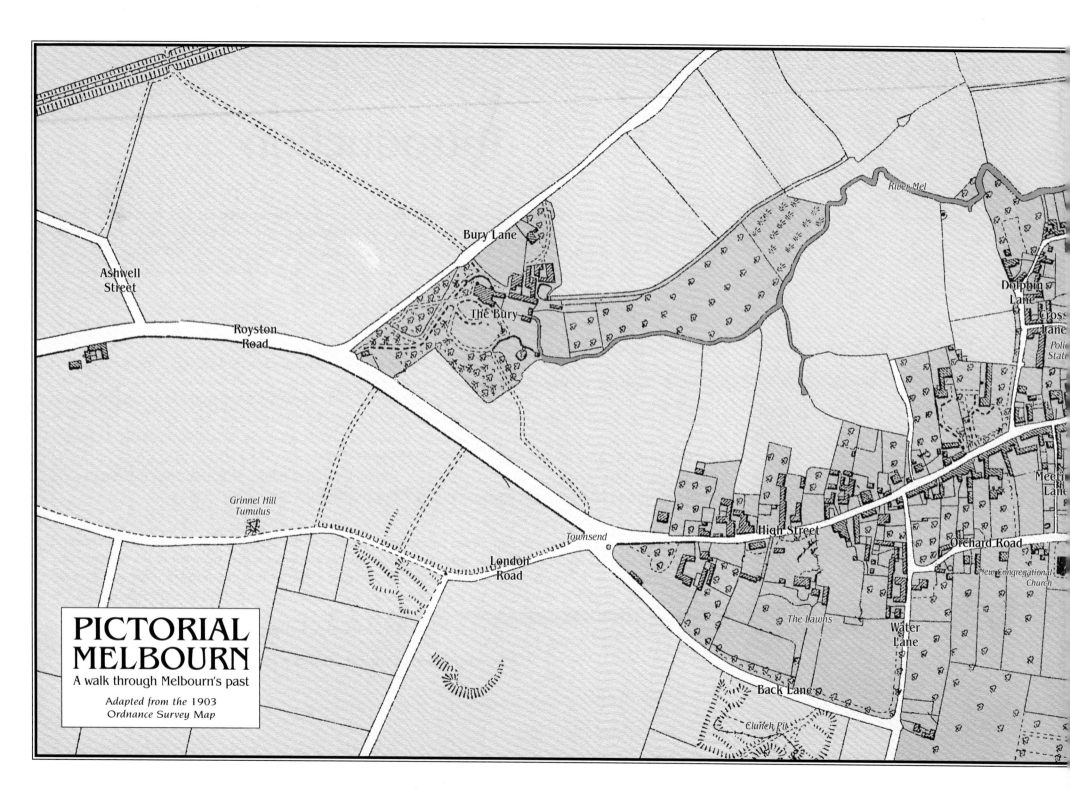

Bury Lane

Ashwell
Street

Royston
Road

The Bury

River Mel

Dolphin
Lane

Cross
Lane

Police
Station

Grinnel Hill
Tumulus

Townsend

High Street

Meeting
Lane

London
Road

Orchard Road

New Congregational
Church

The Lawns

Water
Lane

**PICTORIAL
MELBOURN**

A walk through Melbourn's past

Adapted from the 1903
Ordnance Survey Map

Back Lane

Church Pit

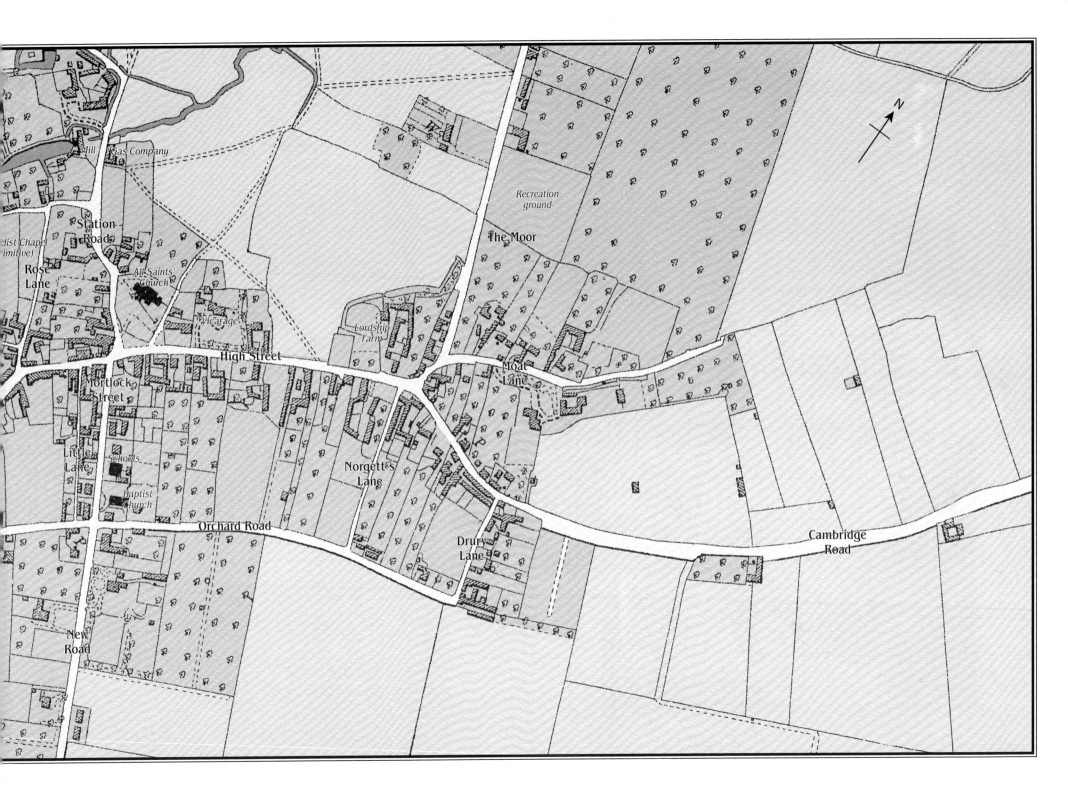

Mill

Gas Company

dist Chapel
imitive)

Station
Road

Rose
Lane

All Saints
Church

Vicarage

Lordship
Farm

Recreation
ground

The Moor

High Street

Moat
Lane

Mortlock
Street

Little
Lane

Schools

Norgett's
Lane

Baptist
Church

Orchard Road

Drury
Lane

Cambridge
Road

New
Road

N

top left: **Tumulus at Grinnel Hill 1936**

top right: **Old London Road, part of Drift Way 1936** (reputed to be the scene of the first meeting between Dick Turpin and Tom King)

bottom left, right and opposite: **Ashwell Street (Strett) 1939**

South of the village

clockwise, from the left:
The Shant public house 1930;
Holland Hall; farmworker's
cottages at Holland Hall 1949;
Fuller's bungalow 1949

11

clockwise, from top left: Bury Lane looking towards Meldreth 1939; back view of the Lodge 1949; Bury Lane looking towards Royston Road 1939

opposite page: The Lodge 1949

Melbourn Bury

Views of The Bury

opposite page, top left and right: The rear of The Bury 1932,
reputed to be from the Tudor period

The springs at The Bury and the source of the River Mel

top right and opposite: During alterations in 1897

Fordham family portraits –
Mrs A.R. Fordham and children, *top right*

bottom left: Temperance Garden Party

opposite page, clockwise from top left: The Fordham family and servants pictured for the 1891 census; Ed Stockbridge and Alfred King, gardeners; The Bury staff; the 1901 census

The interior

top left: The drawing room 1891 and *bottom left* 1907 *bottom right*: The table believed to have been in the Bury since 1539

top right: a painting of The Bury drawn by R.B. Harraden early 1800s

Townsend

bottom right: Devil's Hole, this was at one time a pond.
It used to take a lot of the drainage from Drift Way

clockwise from top left: Elmhurst; The Lawns 1937 (later converted into flats and opened up for evacuees during the war); farm cottages 1929; the High Street

opposite page: Townsend 1936

clockwise from the left: The High Street looking towards The Oak public house; The Locomotive Inn 1932, originally the stables of the Manor belonging to Dame Mary Hatton and pictured again in 1927

opposite page: Trayles Manor 1932, once inhabited by Mary Hatton and much later by Sir Sydney and Lady Harmer

Views, front and rear of Trayles Manor in 1927

opposite page: Greenbanks on the right of the picture, the one time home of the village doctor

Views front (1933) and rear (1935) of Greenbanks, commonly known as 'Dr Gregor's house' and later owned by Dr Hall.

left: The barns at Greenbanks 1935, used as an 'Academy for young gentlemen' run by Dr William Carver (Congregational minister) who once lived at the house. The school was also in a room at the back of the house

clockwise from top left: Milestone house on the left
1929; Sgt Salmons outside Milestone house;
The long wall on the left of Old Farm 1936

The corner of Water Lane

left: High Street, the White Horse public house in the centre

clockwise from top left: Last remains of a thatched wall; the corner 1931 and below in 1952 (front cottage removed); Water Lane looking towards the High Street 1927

Water Lane

opposite page, clockwise from top left:
Corner of Water Lane 1939;
Hop Mallion 1949 (formerly
Dame School); Woodway 1949
(formerly part of Greenbank's
meadows); looking towards the
High Street 1939

left: Wood Lane (also known as
The Drift, now top of Water
Lane); two views of Back Lane
1939 (Lover's Lane)

above: Moss Huggins' public house also known as the Red Cow

right: Albert Huggins, pork butcher outside his brother's pub

opposite page: Looking south along the High Street, Buchan's shop on the left

top left: 'Dubby' Smith's sweet shop, 1931

above: 'Dubby' Smith's' and the Red Cow

bottom right: Looking south towards the Dolphin public house

bottom centre: The Dolphin public house and Haggers' shop 1952

opposite page: Looking northwards towards the Dolphin, with entrance to Mulberry Hall and The Lodge in the centre

top left: **From the High Street 1939**
top right: **South End 1949**
bottom right: **Pear Tree Cottage 1936**

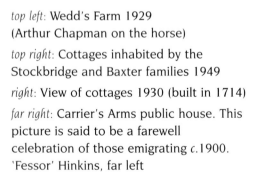

top left: Wedd's Farm 1929
(Arthur Chapman on the horse)

top right: Cottages inhabited by the
Stockbridge and Baxter families 1949

right: View of cottages 1930 (built in 1714)

far right: Carrier's Arms public house. This
picture is said to be a farewell
celebration of those emigrating *c*.1900.
'Fessor' Hinkins, far left

opposite page, top and bottom far left: The Carrier's Arms public house

top left: Former Methodist Chapel and home to the Salvation Army 1949

bottom right: Salvation Army band

clockwise from top left: Croxall's 1949; three views taken in 1936, 1945 and Betty Harrup collecting horse manure in 1936

45

opposite page, top and bottom far left: Catley's 1936
top and bottom right: Stanford's Cottage, 1935
(top) and 1949 (bottom)
this page, top left: Holland's Row 1949
bottom right: Clear's Row 1936

top left: Taken in 1949

top right and bottom left: Burton's Cottage, 1936

bottom right: Dolphin Lane from Station Road

opposite page: Home of the last sheep stealer to be transported to Australia. Photo taken in 1936

After the fire in Dolphin Lane May, 1915.
Photographs from newspaper article of the day

17th century cottages
in Rose Lane, 1939

Rose Lane

top left: Smith's Cottages 1949

top centre: Corner House

top right and bottom left: Cross Lane in 1939

opposite page: Sgt Barrett and PC Conell

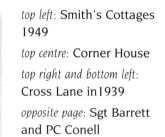

Cross Lane

top left and right: The tuck shop 1926

bottom right: Corner of Meeting Lane on the left

bottom left: At the entrance of Meeting Lane 1936

opposite page: A Huggins butcher's shop and The Hoops

Views of Meeting Lane

centre and top right: looking towards the High Street 1920 *right*: from the High Street *above*: 1928 and *top left*: 1920

opposite page: Three photographs of the old barn, once the Primitive Methodist Chapel *left*:1936 *top right*:1920 *bottom*:1949, demolished 1951

Meeting Lane

top right: York house on the left 1928

bottom left: G A Ward's workshop

bottom right: The back of Ward's workshop

High Street   59

top left: Sketch of the High Street, 1900

right: A closer view of The Hoops public house

right: The Hoops and Huggins' butchers shop

top right: Taken in 1928

Views of the 'old medicine woman's' house 1929

bottom right: Taken in 1928

bottom left: Sgt Charles Salmon

Views of Barns cottage

top right: Barron's Cottage to the rear 1952

bottom right: Thatcher Stanford 1934

bottom left: Thompson's sweet shop 1928

clockwise from top left: Looking towards the Cross, British Legion on the right; Loom's shop 1939; The Rose Inn 1938

opposite page: Farrier's and General Smiths' on the left, old Manor House on the right

The Manor House, front and rear

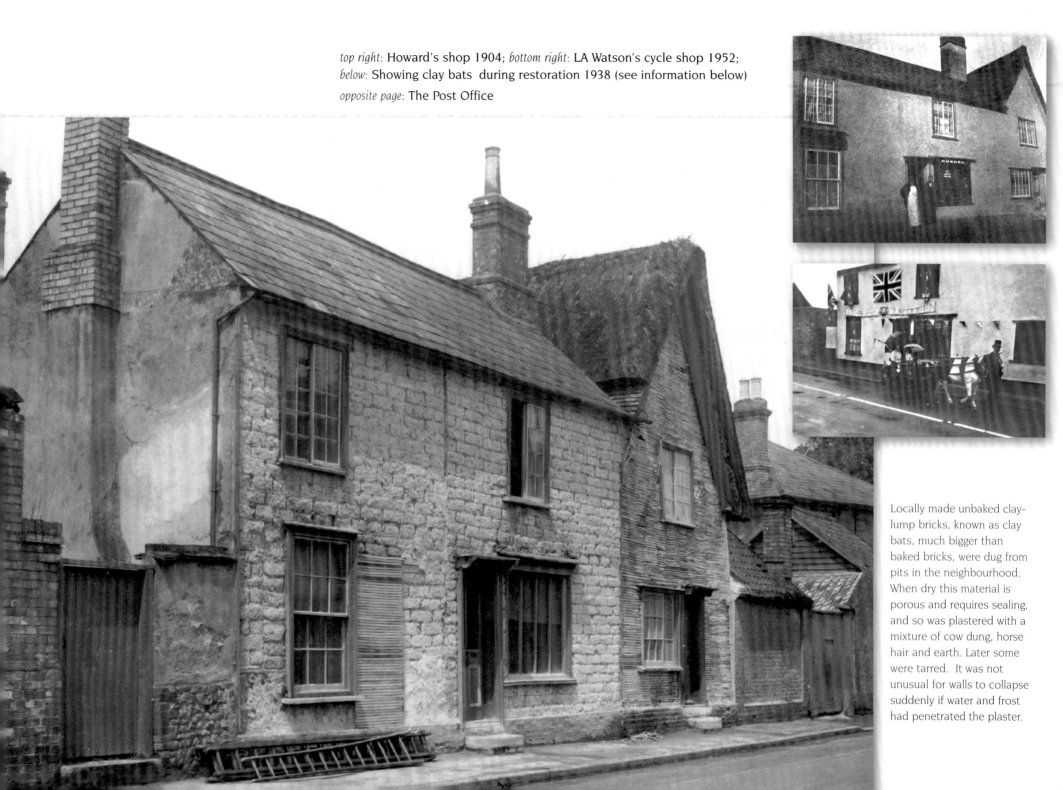

top right: **Howard's shop 1904;** *bottom right*: **LA Watson's cycle shop 1952;**
below: **Showing clay bats during restoration 1938 (see information below)**
opposite page: **The Post Office**

Locally made unbaked clay-lump bricks, known as clay bats, much bigger than baked bricks, were dug from pits in the neighbourhood. When dry this material is porous and requires sealing, and so was plastered with a mixture of cow dung, horse hair and earth. Later some were tarred. It was not unusual for walls to collapse suddenly if water and frost had penetrated the plaster.

The Post Office

opposite page: As A T Lee's

top left and bottom left:
As Cranfield's

top right: As Ralph Ixer's

below: Looking towards
the High Street

clockwise from bottom left:
Cranfield's Post Office;
looking towards the
Cross; the corner of
Little Lane 1929;
'Fesser' Hinkins
outside his shop

opposite page: Little
Lane 1939

74

Little Lane

clockwise, from top: A view taken in 1952; three photographs of Hinkin's house – bottom right taken in 1936

opposite page, top right: Taken in 1936

bottom right: 1935

left: 1936

top left: Restoration of the White Lion after an accident

bottom right: Taken in 1926

top left: Frank Stockbridge's shop adjacent to the Post Office with Loom's haberdashery shop next door

top right: Taken in 1949

bottom right: The deteriorating White Lion

High Street

Accidents at the Cross, outside the White Lion
and Disbury's (butchers)

bottom left: The White Lion following an
accident in 1930

Three views of the Co-op and *above*, its deterioration

top right: The Cross from the Churchyard

The war memorial 1927

Looking south from the Church tower in 1931

above: The last oil lamp

right: Woods' Hygenic Bakery

right: Virginia Cottage 1922

left: Taken from the garden of Virginia cottage

opposite page, clockwise from top left: Farm cottages 1932; Taken in 1931; Melbourn schools; Church Lane in 1908

below: Village water pump outside the schools. This artesian well was dug in *c.*1912 and provided drinking water for the schools and the village

School photographs *far left*: Taken in 1898

School photographs

above right: Taken in 1905

below right: 1920s

95

Right top and bottom: School staff

main picture and above: The Baptist Chapel built
*c.*1857 to replace the building close to the
Red Lion public house; *right*: Taken in 1938

100

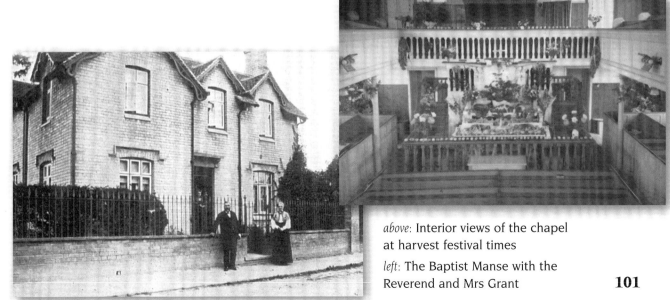

above: Interior views of the chapel at harvest festival times

left: The Baptist Manse with the Reverend and Mrs Grant

101

top left: Clear's almshouses 1949

top right: Homefield 1949

bottom right: 1939

bottom left: 1939

opposite page: Apple Tree Cottage 1931

102 Orchard Road
(formerly Back Lane and Meeting House Road)

The old Independent Chapel

above: Taken in 1939

opposite page, main picture: the interior of the New Congregational Chapel

top right: The parliament clock inside the old chapel 1937

bottom right: An illustration of the new chapel

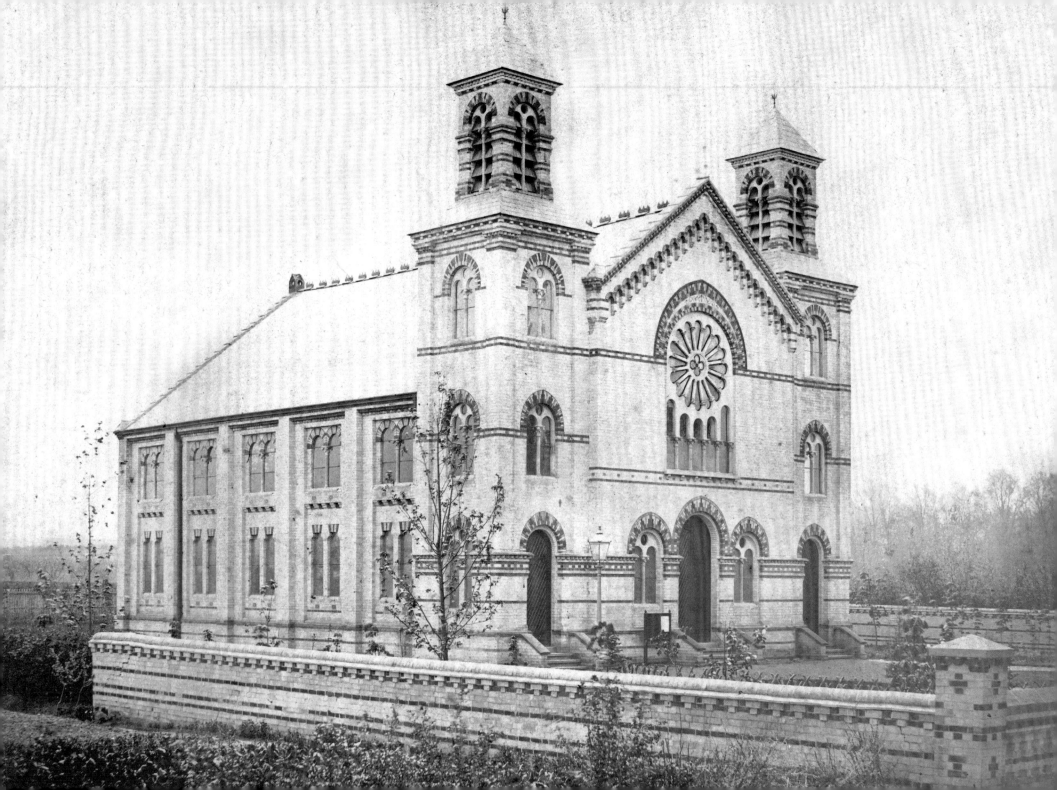

The new Congregational Chapel 1937

above: The new chapel in disrepair

opposite page, top: Taken in 1928

Celebrations for the
Congregational Chapel
bi-centenary bazaar
1894

below: The Black Horse public house 1949
top right: Entrance to Meeting Lane
far right: Along Orchard Road

above: Corner of Water Lane and Orchard Road 1922

below left: 1939

top left: Taken in 1949

top right: Glove Lodge 1949

bottom right: Entrance to the cemetery

bottom left: 1939

115

top right: **Corner of Metcalfe Way**; *main picture insets left*: 1949 *right*: 1952

opposite page, top left: **Flood's cottage 1949**

bottom left: **Ebbisham Cottage 1949**

opposite page and above left: Primrose House
bottom right: The Congregational Manse
bottom left: opposite the Baptist Manse

Three views of New Road in 1952

bottom left: New Road Farm 1952

opposite page: New Road looking towards the Church

above and left: Summerhouse Farm 1949

clockwise from top left: Hyde Hill Farm 1929; Heath Farm cottages 1949 (*and right centre*); Heath Farm 1949; Hillside Poultry Farm 1949

top left and right: Heath Farm showing windmill (top right 1929)

bottom right: Noon's Folly; Grange Farm 1929

left and above: **The Coach and Horses at Flint Cross**
right: **Wedd's garage 1949**
bottom right: **The Haven**
bottom left: **North Hall School 1939**

Memorial services at the Cross

bottom left and right: Armistice Day service in 1935

opposite page: The Café, Newmarket Road 1949

All Saints' Church

right: Jubal Howard with his baker's basket

bottom right: Haymaking in the Churchyard

top right: Wedding 1929

bottom left: Milly Catley's funeral *c*.1932

opposite page: An early photograph of the Church *c*.1865

The Church was the most photographed building in the village. The many examples that follow may look similar, but subtle differences can be seen. Note the photographs taken before the memorial was erected.

PARISH CHURCH, MELBOURN

opposite page: The Old Elm Tree

top left: South side of the Church and George Bullen

top right: A point in the wall where a gateway stood, used by the Lord of the Manor on his way to Church. It was his privilege to own a right of way in a straight line from his Manor direct to the Church porch

bottom right: The porch 1932. The Parvis Chamber over the porch accommodated one of the first schools in the country

clockwise from left: The Old Elm Tree in 1914; From a painting by R.B. Harraden; The Old Elm Tree in the late 1800s

opposite page: Postcard of a painting of the Church and Elm Tree; Benjamin Metcalfe's gravestone; Hawkes' family tombs 1937

The Old Elm Tree and
Church at Melbourn A.D. 1851

147

opposite and top left: Return of six re-cast bells 1913

bottom left: Screen to tower vestry in memorial of Cranfield

150

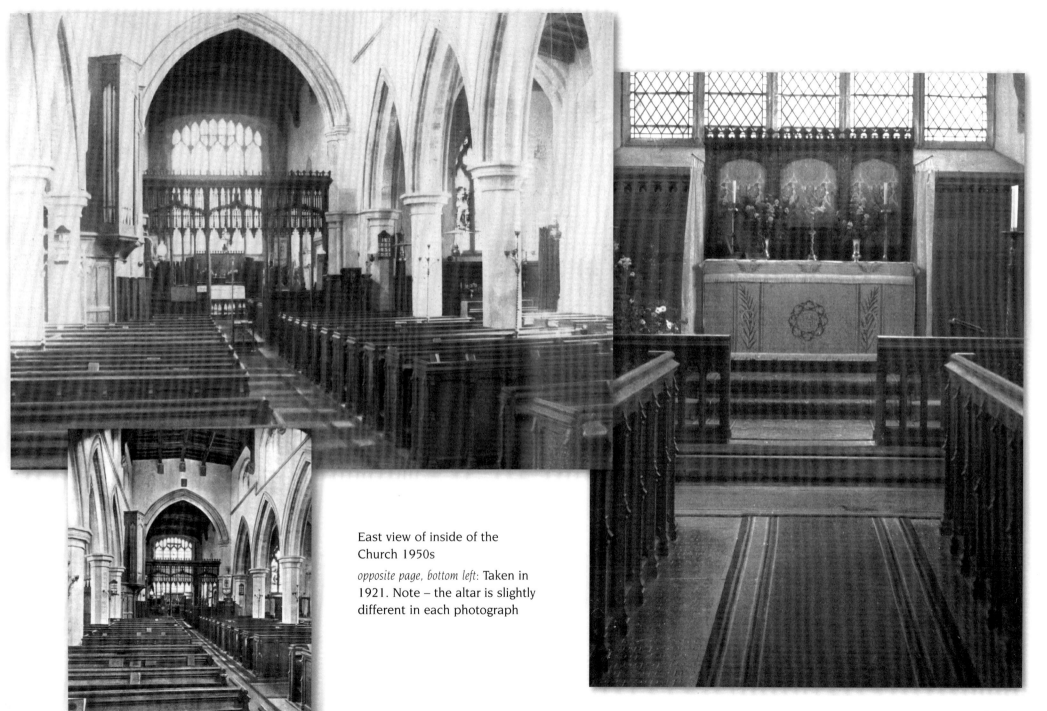

East view of inside of the
Church 1950s

opposite page, bottom left: Taken in
1921. Note – the altar is slightly
different in each photograph

The Lady Chapel (Chapel of St Mary also known as the Argentine Chapel)

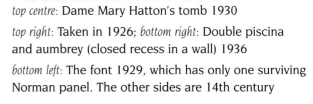

top centre: Dame Mary Hatton's tomb 1930

top right: Taken in 1926; *bottom right*: Double piscina and aumbrey (closed recess in a wall) 1936

bottom left: The font 1929, which has only one surviving Norman panel. The other sides are 14th century

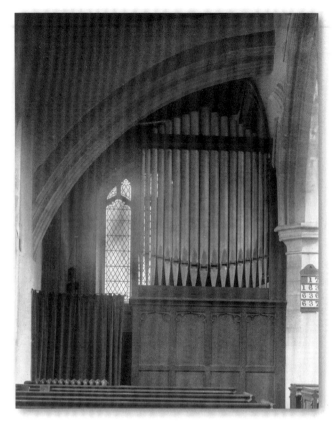

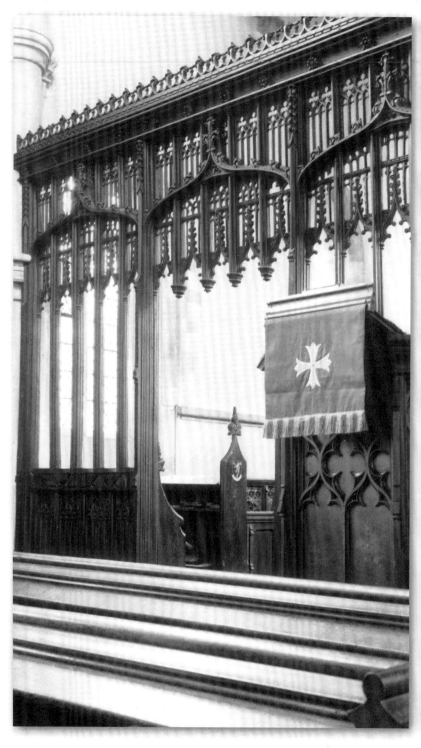

above: Chapel of The Holy Trinity

far right: The rood screen

bottom centre: North aisle 1926

opposite page: Vicarage Meadows (also known as Church or Glebe Meadows)

154

The Meadows 157

Looking south from the Church Tower. Note the Independent Chapel in the background 1930

(formerly Mill Lane)

top left: South Cambs
Electrical Co. on the
left in 1939

bottom right: 1927

bottom left: 1941

top left: Chapman's shop; *top right*: Earlier picture showing Campkin's grocer and hardware shop 1927; *bottom right*: Campkin's 1932

Views of Station Road
clockwise from top left: Taken in 1938; 1936; early 1930s
opposite page, top right: Stockbridge Cottage in the centre 1934

top right: Taken in 1930

bottom right: Joseph Stockbridge with horse and cart

opposite page: Taken in 1949

169

clockwise from top left: Side view of Hales, building contractor and decorator, taken in 1935; Melbourn fire engine house 1935

opposite page: Hales in 1927

172

opposite page, clockwise from top left: Holland's house; taken in 1927; 1927; 1949

this page, top left and bottom centre: Ellis' (blacksmiths) 1939

top right: Coningsby's 1949

bottom right: Corner of Dolphin Lane

top left: Riverside House 1949 (site of the steam laundry)

top right: Brown's foundry 1949 (site of the Gas company and at one time Groves Shoe Shop)

right: Turner's shop on the right 1949 (Granny Hinkins sold sweets here)

opposite: Mill House

Sheene Mill

top right: Inside the mill 1930, showing the apple wood cogs

bottom left: One of the grindstones 1934

bottom right: Side view of the Mill taken in 1929

clockwise from top left: Cowslip Corner; The
Meads; path to the station; The Meads
opposite page: Sheene Mill

183

left: The kissing gate; *above*: The Meads, beyond Mill Lane

Cowslip Corner
*Other names have been used, this
one is the more polite version!*

above: Postcard of BR poster depicting Melbourn

top and bottom right: Meldreth and Melbourn Station

opposite page: The Cross

top right: The memorial in 1934

opposite page, top left: Horse manure sweepers 1932

top right: Old barn at the Cross; *bottom right*: The barn converted. It later became Howard's bakery shop. Jubal Howard also had a museum in this building

The Passive Resistance Sale 1905

bottom left: Taken in 1930

bottom right: Muncey's cows being taken down to Moat Meadows

top left: Public houses, The Anchor (centre)
and The Elm Tree (on the right)

opposite page: The Anchor 1905

clockwise from top left: The Anchor 1939; corner of the Churchyard 1928 showing Arthur Bullen; The old vicarage

201

above: The Old Elm Tree

top right and far right: Tea room at the old vicarage

bottom left: The Stockbridge Farm

above: The Vicarage (*top*: 1949)

right: The High Street, Wood's Farm in centre 1910

top right: Taken in 1949

bottom right: Thompson's garage 1927. The building to the left of the garage was previously the Spotted Dog public house

Woods Farm

opposite page, top left: 1930 A blocked up window was exempt from the window tax providing it displayed a visible notice below it.

top right: In celebration of the new Queen 1952

One of the largest barns was used by the whole village for a feast to celebrate the coronation of Queen Victoria.

this page, bottom right: The cheese room

opposite page: Wood's Farm from Lordship Farm

top left: Bill Wilson outside Wood's Farm

Lordship Farm (*top left*: 1930)

bottom right: The garden

bottom centre: Hall of John de Argentine 1924

above: The Star public house 1932; *opposite page*: Herbert and Lizzie King at White House Farm

White House Farm

top left: the Vellum family; *bottom left*: 1949

bottom right: Farm Corner 1936 and *opposite*: Muncey family

Stockbridge Farm
(Farm Corner)

opposite page: from 1926 to
1934. The deterioration
of a cottage in Norgett's
Lane

pages 216–217: Moor Corner
Howard's bakery and house.
Three views on this page
taken in 1949.

top left: Corner of Moat Lane showing Robinson's Tailors shop

top right: The Poplars 1930; *bottom right:* 1936

top right: Moat House 1935

three views this page 1939 and opposite page: Newlings Farm (also known as Whitings)

opposite page, top far left: Long Thatch 1933; *top and bottom 2 pictures*: Rawlings Foundry 1939

this page, top left: Moat Lane corner *left*: Stanford's

top left: Stanford's
bottom left: Taken in 1939
far right: Nightingale's
shop on left

opposite, top right: Stanford's house; *above*: Blacksmith's 1937

Four views of The Red Lion public house
built in 1659 – demolished 1937

far left: The Red Lion owned by Thomas Wedd, (*above*: 1937)

Five views of Sheepshead Row *opposite page, right*: the rear

clockwise from top left: **Drury Lane in 1949; 1938; 1938; Hale's house 1933**

opposite: Abrey's shop with Maggie Stanford and son Edwin on the left and Daisy Abrey

opposite page, clockwise from top left: Portway 1949; The Cherries 1949; The Bull's Head public house

clockwise from top left: Rumby's bungalow 1949; Langdale; Ansell's 1949; Whinscroft 1949; Godfrey's Farm 1936; Basham's and Wisbey's 1949;

centre: Cherry Park 1950s;

clockwise from above: Taylor's 1949; Foxfield Farm 1932; cottage at Black Peak Farm 1932; Watercress beds near Black Peak 1925

Restoration

The quality of many of these photographs featured in this book came to us in very good condition. Others were marked, although with a little extra work, water spots, scratches and the odd pen marks were easily removed.

The collection of images here show that the appearance of a poor quality picture doesn't mean that the detail cannot be enhanced to its former glory.

These two photographs show that some photographs have more to offer than first appears. The picture on the right is in its original state when scanned in. With the use of modern day equipment the detail can be revealed as shown below.

The picture above right had not aged well. The faded sepia colour, the detail hardly discernible, it was marked with pen. Below shows the picture restored.

Many of the photographs found in this book have have been reproduced from old postcards, some dating to the late 1800s. Some postcards are copies of original photographs, although in some instances the reproduction is copied, and each subsequent image recopied – until the detail is lost. Below are two views of the High Street, the top picture is an unrestored original photo (see page 67) whilst the one at the bottom is a copy. Note the bottom copy has not been reproduced from the one above as can be seen by the trim.

We have been very fortunate in that few of the photographs we received were badly damaged, but as you can see here those that have been scratched or torn can often be restored to their original condition.

It is important to preserve these treasures for future generations

Since the invention of the camera in the mid 1800s, photographs have made an important contribution in recording our past. They freeze in time those moments that have important meaning to both the memory of the individual and the community alike. Photographs are often taken at local meetings and fetes while there is little or no written record to augment the event.

No matter what the quality, most pictures can be restored and kept in ways that will preserve them forever. Deposits made to local archives and museums are always welcomed.